"James Benger has long been a voice for the down and out, those who've never caught a break or had that one teacher who took notice and said, "You can do this." Most of the world looks away from them. Benger shows us their pain and humanity, pulls us into their corner. She, the subject of this collection, is never named. Is she you? Have you been through a bad patch when you wished for anything but this anything? She's paralyzed in endless self-talk, all colors bleeding to gray. No lust tomorrow / can grow / with her thumb / on life's reset. Dear reader, please put out your hand and help her to the other side."

-Alarie Tennille, author of *Three A.M. at the Museum* and *Waking on the Moon.*

"James Benger's work consistently shines in its intimacy, bringing insight and understanding to bear upon the lives of those mostly forgotten or discarded by time and polite society. on the edge of something is no exception to this rule. Each poem reads like an encapsulated novel. The great joy of this work negates the unlikelihood that this voice would be heard in their brutal existence, clinging in dank solitary to their last rays of sunlight and hope. James gives emotions context and life in a way that immortalizes each of these experiences and should exalt these voices to the echelon of the beauty of human experience that they always deserved."

-Macey Web, author of *Crying at Walls*

Previous publications by James Benger

poetry:

Rust Stain Reality (2025 Alien Buddha Press)
About Those Losses (with Sarah Worrel and Lindsey
Martin-Bowen) (2024 Spartan Press)
Waiting on Hummingbirds (with Jason Baldinger) (2024
Kung Fu Treachery Press)
Floating Downstream (2024 LAB 52)
Ravenous and Salivating (with Sarah Worrel) (2022
DroneBEE Gazette)
This Still Life (with Jason Baldinger) (2021 Kung Fu
Treachery Press)
Misfits in the Front Row (with Sarah Worrel) (2021 Kung
Fu Treachery Press)
From the Back (2020 Spartan Press)
Things Have Changed (2019 Dark Particle Press)
Everyone's Alone Tonight (with Jason Baldinger) (2019
Kung Fu Treachery Press)
The Park (2019 Kelsay Books)
Against the Dark (with Tyler Robert Sheldon) (2019
Stubborn Mule Press)
Little Fires Hiding (with Jason Baldinger) (2018 Kung Fu
Treachery Press)
You've Heard it All Before (2017 GigaPoem)
As I Watch You Fade (2016 EMP)

fiction:

One Week (2025 Alien Buddha Press)
Jack of Diamonds (2013 LAB 52)
Flight 776 (2012 LAB 52)

on the edge of something

poems by James Benger

Luchador Press
Big Tuna, Texas

Copyright © James Benger, 2026
First Edition: 1 3 5 7 9 10 8 6 4 2
ISBN: 979-8-89975-044-1
LCCN: 2026939222

Front cover photo: Stefano Pollio
Back cover photo: Jetbu
Interior photo: Mitch
Author photo: Marcia Epstein

Acknowledgments:

The author would like to thank all the publishers who gave many of these poems their first home, Jason Ryberg at Spartan Press for giving this book a home, Jason Baldinger, and Sarah Worrel both of whom continue to collaborate with me, Alarie Tennille for reading, blurbing, and suggesting a better title, Macey Webb for reading an early version and providing invaluable feedback and a blurb, anyone who reads my books, the 365 Poems in 365 Days online workshop, and as always, Dad, Hannah, Milo, and Felix.

For everyone I've forgotten, you know who you are. I'll get you next time. Several of the poems in this collection originally appeared in various forms in the following publications:

Angel's Share
The Beatnik Cowboy
Gasconade Review
Heartland!
Hooligan Street Poetry
Horror Sleaze Trash
impspired
I-70 Review
Lothlorien Poetry Journal
North of Oxford
Orenaug Poetry Journal
River Dog
Sola Poeta
Thimble Literary Magazine
Thorny Locust
Words Save Lives
365 Days

Table of Contents

For anyone who finds hope.

This world is not my home,
I'm just passing through.

-Jim Reeves, *This World is Not My Home*

on the edge of something

she waits at the window

time passes
passes
passes
she doesn't notice

she waits at the window
days are days
but this is life
this is real
this is all

she waits at the window
it will all make sense
it will
all things will eventually
add up

she waits at the window
and life keeps extrapolating
for everyone
but her

magic

she forcibly sees things in clouds

any number of wonders
deities
aliens
illustrations of the kama sutra
her great aunt
nothing is off limits
when imagination
and more importantly
hope
are the only weapons

she forcibly sees things in clouds
she has to
because there's no magic to be found
anywhere else

seconds

days come down on her
the malice of the world
or of herself
she doesn't know
doesn't care
the end result is the same

the world seems to be
bent on killing her
or maybe she is
but it doesn't matter
the end result is the same

the days come down on her
tie her bind her
trap her within herself
promise nothing but
slow painful decay

the days the hours
they do this

but there are minutes
sometimes only seconds
when she feels like
she imagines the rest of the
world feels

and despite all the days
the seconds will save her

muddling

she's searching for
any reason
to keep this going

because the mud
keeps getting deeper
and her legs are
so tired

and there never seems
to be any end
no foreseeable reward

only endless muddling
to go and go and go
wearing her pencil down
to the last useless nub

a flower
pressed and pressed and pressed
until it's nothing but
an impotent powder of blandness

she's searching
and moving
and only half hoping
her legs don't give out

dry

let it all drain you
it's going to do it
anyway
so might as well make it easier
give up
and let it happen

that's what she tells herself
as the door goes unanswered
and the tub has been dry
longer than memory

nothing seems worthwhile
other than the
absolute
minimum

the cars outside
with their belligerent horns
and the children with their
cries and screams
their laughter
it all seems so foreign

but just familiar enough
that maybe it's something she knew
in a life
that came before
this

wishes

this is something
she spends most of her time
trying to forget

the festering memories
dripping from her fingertips
the moldering remnants as
of all those yesterdays
fall into the gutters
of all these tomorrows

this cyclical existence
brings her back to this
ghost of herself
again
and again
and again

she often wishes for many things
but most days
above it all
she wants a tomorrow
free of today

her untitled day

she sits by her window
drawn dark and cold
imagining the life
that could be
signaling to herself
possibilities left to atrophy

she almost saw the
sunset yesterday
but it was too much
to open the blinds
and actually look
out onto a world
she often wishes would
annex itself from
her existence

these are her days and nights
a life comprised of
the only compromise
she could ever tolerate
a wholly insular life
in exchange for shunning
an unyielding world

she's not sure when was
the last time she ate

much less bathed
she hasn't checked the mailbox
down the hall in weeks
though she can't imagine
it contains anything important

a siren wails through the
thin walls from somewhere
down the crumbling street

perhaps tonight
she will sleep

abandoned abandon

she finds this world
blanketed in yesterdays
and willfully forgotten
instances of regret

last moments
before the blinds close
her misplaced abandon

hollow

her days bleed into nights
and they all consist of
trading hands with herself
interchanging responsibility
with culpability
and it all weighs more than
what's left of her will to stand
can hold up to in these
her most hollow times

she shuffles to anything
that might prove an answer
or at least a road to
anything else
but it all comes back to
a spiral into the dirt's subbasement

sometimes she wants that
floral patterned bathroom wallpaper life
that she remembers her grandmother having
all cheerful frugality
and no not a single observable regret
but she knows these memories
aren't real at least not to anyone
save what's left of her childhood

someone down the hall fries bacon
and she doesn't know why
the smell
the thought of preparing a meal
the thought of creating anything
worthy of sustaining life
is something to praise
when she feels nothing but nausea

the cabinets are empty
and someone shouts something unkind
on the other side of her
shuttered and barred window
and she feels a sick kinship
with the madness
in the least whimsical way possible

she doesn't know the day
much less the time
but it's not like at this point
any of that matters

twist

she does her best
to bend her brain
contort her perception

into something approaching
a shape that could make this
close to acceptable

the days pile up
into nothing but this
and this is less every day

but she repeatedly finds a light
when she wakes to see the results
of a two a m snowfall

the cold sterile perfection
outside her freezing window
gives her something to strive for

and all the mental gymnastics
could never amount
to those moments

rot

the days crawl on
with a monotonous rapidity

that she wouldn't mind so much
but it's the ball of acid
that leeches from her guts
to everything
eyeballs and fingertips
lips and soul

it tells her as it burns
nothing
nothing
no

just once
she would like to hear the
bright glowing affirmative
come from inside
the cooling comfort
of internal approval

the alarm blares hell

as every morning
she stares at the ceiling
holds her breath
hopes that today won't be
like all the others

pull

she finds herself wondering
what is all this
is this really what it is
it certainly can't be
all there is

she finds herself
thinking these things
and dreaming of some kind of
hopeful obsession
that will take her
away from all of this
longing and low grade dullness
the swimming persistent nagging
of something more
something perpetually out of reach

something to pull her out
and keep her out

light switch

she admits that these moments
have balled her into herself
forcing everything inside
to condense and calcify
a pit of bitter acid
burning in her soul
threatening to metastasize
and release its poisoning toxin
throughout all that she is
or was
and jeopardizing
all that she might be

if only the noise could
stop
just for a day
or even a few minutes
to help her regain
a footing that now seems
largely forgotten
in the carbon copy pages
of this rolodex life

rain falls outside the window
and in here
she's dry and warm
physically

but she feels everything else
everything that counts
moldering to soft obsolescence
and crumbling under the gravity
that all those other bodies
seem to effortlessly withstand

no need to turn on the lights today

she calls it her talent

this ability to
take the world of the day
and in seconds
raze it like one would
a moldering building
that has become
a festering tooth
in the jawline of a street

it's her willingness
to erase
negate
prove all to herself
to be
undesirable
unnecessary
expendable

nearly every night now
she exercises this
muscle of subtraction
believing it to be
temporary and fluid

no suspense
no lust for tomorrow
can grow
with her thumb
on life's reset

she finds a reason

she finds a reason
and life moves on
long monotonous
continuous life

she finds a reason
to forget all those things
that were so so important
and life moves on

she finds a reason
to neglect all the things
that once moved her
and life moves on

she finds a reason
to never again dance
in the dark to that song
they both loved so much
once upon a lifetime
and life moves on

she finds a reason
to never touch those books
on the shelf all dusty
regal and antique
and life moves on

she finds a reason
to refrain from running
through the streets, aimless
and divine at 3 a.m.
and life moves on

she finds a reason
to pretend that she never
really cared about any of
these things that once
defined her
and life moves on

she finds a reason
to forget and because
she found that reason
life never moved on

the slide

most nights
she's perfectly content
to fold in on herself
swallow herself
negate herself

perhaps content
is the wrong word
but that perpetual cycle
of denying all inside
is nothing if not
familiar
which seems almost
comfortable

she'd draw the blinds
if they were ever open
she'd turn off the phone
but no one ever calls

it's all darkness
it's all hopeless
and she's seen it all before

she once pretended that
when the others' sun came
when she opened her eyes

things would look different
but she's grown too old and tired
for such childish fantasies

she'd punch a wall in frustration
but what would that change

she's beginning to lose her grip
on the difference between
day and night
and she's knows it

but she's not sure
it really matters

edge

she sleeps on the
edge of the mattress
never intends to
that's just where she always is
when she wakes up
doesn't matter much
not like that mattress is on
anything higher than the ground

it's been this way for too long
always on the edge of something
but never quite there
always stagnating
never any kind of
cleansing resurgence

the cigarettes are stale
the subway piss is stale
the exhaust always
looming in the air is stale
the tips at the club are stale
the men's half assed
entitled advances are stale
the lonely bourbon afterward is stale
the edge of the mattress is stale
everything about life is

so much so
she begins to wonder if maybe
it's not life
but her

she thinks she can remember a time
when things made sense
and when they didn't
it didn't matter
because it really didn't

now nothing adds up
and everything matters
and nothing is right
and she's not sure she understands
the words clean and fresh

sunrise

every day
she promises to renew
to bring herself
back to home
and begin again
pretend that all this
never happened

the relief upon waking
and knowing
that nightmare
was just that
and the sun is
only now rising
and nothing
needs to be righted
because nothing
was ever wrong

she promises herself
that blank slate
that pure white page
that scarless life
and she knows
it could be right there

but every morning
as the sun begins its dance
to ignite the day
she flounders
and finds yesterday
under the coffee coaster
and it bites hard
and all she can hope for
is the next tomorrow

free

she finds some kind of
perverse comfort
in the endless hours of
almost assuredly hopeless
waiting

there's an unspoken promise
hiding in the dark corners of
the unknown
a promise
or at least
not an
outright denial

so she waits patiently
in the furthest darkest
reaches of herself
knowing full well that
whatever comes
could be worse
but just perhaps
it will change everything
and she'll finally be free

riverbed

she floats downstream
on the current of herself
riding recursive rivers of
everything that once was
all the moments of the past
return to remind her of the
wrong choice
missed opportunity
failed test
and these moments
these raindrops
culminate in a rapid flow
unremittingly surging toward
total final decline

something undetectable
has remained her raft
throughout all of this
for so long
something unnamable
yet she's been sensing
pinpricks
only a few at first
but now the air is rushing
warning bubbles in the water
and she knows it won't be long
until she finally joins
the riverbed

talk

occasionally she has to
talk to people
and when that happens
no matter the situation
no matter the transaction
it always boils to
them telling her
that it's not so bad
and she needs to look up
see the sun
the trees
feel the cleanness of the air
rolling around her lungs

and the first few times
when this happened
she maybe believed them
maybe a little
and she tried
but everything
continued to spit in her face
and kick her shins
and remind her that
it will never be more

so now when she hears
all those well meaning platitudes

she has to summon all the
boulders of control
from wherever in her guts
that they live
to not throw hands
or run screaming
or simply jump into traffic

she's getting good at
finding ways to
avoid conversations

after the race

she's running
running
through this
hoping to outlast
whatever is behind

and she's running
out of breath
and running out of steam
and just maybe
running out if herself

so she slows to
staring at her shoes
and only wishing
to stop

she turns on a burning heel
and welcomes
whatever comes next

exhaustion

as if any of this was
planned
ordained

as if this was
what she wanted all along

every day is tired
in a way she understands
hundred year old trees
can be tired

like the salt in the ocean
is tired

like how the last kiss
before the coffin closes
is tired

she walks when she must
which is far more
than she'd like
because she's tired

the streets seem perfunctory
there's a bustle in the sky
in the passersby's

collective obnoxious breath

she can't imagine what
could possibly be so important
as to deny the darkness
that they all must see

they must see
because it's so obvious
it's all around
it's in everything
it's of everything
and even it's tired

tired in the way the sun
grows wary with each moon

keys fitting in locks
like warm deception
tumblers tumbling
granting admittance
like a benevolent hooded figure
before the gallows

she sacrifices herself
upon the altar of life
every day
and everything's getting tired

terminal negation

there's a uselessness to the day
and inexplicable pointlessness
that prods her into inaction

blood runs sluggish in tired veins
and feet on the floor seem like
yesterday's fool's dream

the shower is mostly clean
only a little grime
a little mildew
she's pretty sure soap doesn't go bad

but the energy
the time invested
seems wholly unwarranted

there's that saying about
polishing a turd

a cell phone is a godsend
and enabler of the primally unmotivated
those terminally bound to their
traitor brains

tomorrow that phone on the
scratchy scarred floor
will glow and buzz

and she will say
no

it's been a while since anything

we're always doing everything we can
to forever forget everything

this is what she thinks
as the last drop soaks into her tongue
it would be bitter
if she weren't already so numb

the keys are across the aluminum table
closes an eye to see straight
figures if she can make out
each scratch etched into the metal
each letter in the ancient
grocery store discount fob on the ring
maybe she's together enough
to make it to mexico
or at least make it out of this

the cluster of keys and plastic
blend as her eyes go dry
and she shakes her head
trying to clear
thinking cracking the seal
of the last untouched one on top the microwave

the mattress in the next room calls
but what's the point
what's the goddamn point

there's a butcher knife in the sink
she could leave the door open for the
coyotes or foxes
or fucking maggots

it's been a hot day
and the man on the radio says
tomorrow'll be hotter
with no end in sight
world without end

she closes her eyes
and allows herself the useless hope
for anything

here's the latest

the forecast tells her
all is useless
so pack it in
not only is there no hope
there never was

it was only that persistent rat
at the back of your brain
saying
get back to it
because this is all your fault
and the world suffers
because of you

so get back to it
because everyone's dying
and maybe not so slow anymore

but that was only herself
her deeper self
shutting everything down
and bringing it to boil
as she cooked and dried
withering to something less than

the forecast tells her
all these things

she once thought
must only be from within

she goes to turn off the talking head
but the knob won't click
and the plug's too battle worn
to risk a yank
so she settles for the volume
down to zero
and a holy blanket over the screen

she closes her eyes to the
muffled traffic report
and tries to remember a time
of good news

the practice

they tell her to
find some point on the horizon
and focus on it
to center herself
to bring it all to a
coolly white hot
pebble in the middle
of it all

and some days she finds herself
just low enough to try
but it doesn't matter what she picks
out the filthy window

the grease dog vender on the corner
the fading neon of the strip club
three blocks over
the woman with the stroller
two inches from breakdown
even the hills that can almost be seen
through the haze of exhaust
and dying gasps of atmosphere

distraction to the dusty floorboards
is the only result
and the ember at her core
pitifully smolders

and disseminates
and tomorrow
she'll be even more fractured

partial asphyxia

sometimes
some parts of her
just won't work

there'll be a day
when her legs won't carry
her feet won't support

there'll be a moment
when the fingers
threaten mutiny
refusing to grasp
even the lightest of burdens

there'll be dark hours when
there's nothing but the
incessant dripping of
what she assumes is
the last liquefying remnants
of her soul
leaking out
soaking the stained pillow

there'll be those long nights
when her eyes refuse to obey
and only see the mud and insects
of a world claiming to be

made of sun and joy

there'll be those days when
her skin refuses to feel anything
but the cold of an air
wanting only to be a breath

there'll be those days
those nights
when she's sure
this betrayal will end her

but the next breath comes

marked

she longs for an alteration
any change
to this existence
of tasteless repetition
of all colors
bleeding to grey
of the stained circulars
jammed in the community mailbox
to look like anything other
than a scrapbook killer's
wet dream

she spends sunless hours
trolling neon for meaning
and in the bright
she sees but doesn't understand
the smiles
as if they know something
as if there's some grand scheme
some rule book
and everyone has a copy
beside their pillow
but she's left
to puzzle out the board
feeling like alien hieroglyphics

she's heard that the oxygen's sweet
if you let it be
but she can't see it as anything other than
another gas
just as likely to strangle as sustain

she studies the dirt
under her fingernails
and wonders
if she died right now
would a mortician or anyone
bother to clean them
or would she continue to be
dirty for eternity

perspective

she continues to see all of this
as some bland pale reflection
discount counterfeit life
boiling under a current of
polished masked civility

every moment she feels
the blood pulsing at her temples
and it's getting increasingly difficult
to remember a time when
this bungeed down rage wasn't there
threatening to explode

acidic fang bared aggression
melting humanity to
steaming puddles on the pavement

from her window
she sees them cross the street
oblivious to just how close
to annihilation they all are

the sign at the crosswalk goes red

best of intentions

she used to catch herself
hiding under anything

desks at school
piles of blankets at home
the dilapidated bridge
over the drainage ditch
down by the tracks

anywhere that provided
the slightest bit of cover
any place that might allow her
to not be found
she never knew she was

going to those places
she'd just find herself there
breathing hard and hoping
for some undefinable release
some kind of, not hope

but absence of hopelessness
she no longer finds herself
hiding under anything
but her own shell
her own inevitable hardening

some nights as she's alone
thinking of what might've been
she wonders if this really is
for the best

the factory

she comes here
when there's nothing else

those first
tentative steps
not so long ago
when everything was dark
the rain was freezing
and the gravel surrounding
shifted with every step
threatening to be like all the rest
to try its damnedest
to take her down

she found this place
on a bright cold day
but it is at night
when she chooses to visit
not every night
only when she needs it
and lucky enough
we need it to

there is love in this place
and she doesn't have to look far
beyond the cracked bare concrete floors
the exposed wiring

that saw its last spark
long ago
the scant traces of things
that've come here for refuge
and never left

exchange rate

the nights are long and sweaty
errant cars stream by
their high beams
painting prison bars
through her blinds
onto the bare wall

everything seems to
move slower these days
but the world picks up pace
constantly spinning at a
deceptively higher rate
but it's all she can do
to get from bed before
the sun goes down again
to bring the darkness

save those strobes
reminding her
there are others
who breathe the same air
and yet they seem to get
something more than
mere sustenance
out of the exchange

unspoken

some mornings
when her eyes finally open
the dusty light
filtering through the
cracked blinds
offers a promise of warmth

an avenue to rejoin a collective
that systematically
methodically rejected her
in years of minuscule slights
that pile into a mountain of reasons
to never try again

the phone on the floor rings
for the first time in memory
illuminating the wood paneled walls
in manufactured glow
combining with their
street life sun
oppressing her
and pressing her
deeper into herself

the phone goes dark
the only message
is silence

again

she sees yesterdays
burning in the back

but all that's in front
is the nagging reality

nothing will last
and all of this will crumble

a sea of useless intentions
muffled in the scarred reality
of this bland recurrence

heterokaryon

the floor's never been closer
or that's how she sees it

staring at the blemishes
in the dirty worn wood
the degradation of that floor
seems nothing if not
confirmation of
even the stoutest things'
willingness to compromise
under extreme circumstances

she is those planks
shifting and buckling
with the atmospheric pressure
defacing itself to the will of
steel toe boots
heavy furniture
a dropped anything

she can no longer be certain
but there was possibly
a time before all this inevitability

now she spends hours
stomach down on the mattress
inches from that floor

thinking about
the day when
they finally
become
one

clouds

she remembers a time
when things mattered,
when everything wasn't
always gone

time and days,
people and their plans
all of this made sense
had a place
in the collective everything

she flips back through
old calendars
trying to pinpoint exactly
when it all turned
and became this
grey mist of a life

she wonders if it's a
chemical imbalance
or maybe it's the
rest of the world

she remembers those colors
they were so vivid
so shockingly bright
they could blind a person

if they weren't ready
or at least
shake them to tears

everything smelled like life
everything flowed
moved with easy purpose

she sees the children
on the playground
outside her bedroom window
hears the beautiful cries
the warmth in each movement

she sees the sun
just above the clouds

eyes

there's a dying ember of tomorrow
smoldering in her once brilliant
one electric blue
now red watery despondent eyes

she can almost remember a time
when everything mattered
when all of this was nothing
and everything else
all of the outside of these hours
was much more than simply
something to get through

get through to get where
here
this

this seems less a destination
less a reward
more a prison
constructed by careless frivolity
and inevitable desperation

there's a nagging silent hope
that sometimes claws at the
back of her brain
but she's gotten good at

drowning it down
every time she comes in the door
her self hatred grows a little stronger
She doesn't know she's thought of this
but she has
and maybe if she's lucky
someday she'll realize it

tears threaten to burst
every time she motions
for another
mile marker to familiar blackout

some people are so broken
you never have to share a single word
you can find their whole story
suffocating in their eyes

muzzle

she seethes from inside
trying to imagine what
it must be like
to be one of them

running through the world
with an obnoxious abandon
caution to the cyclone
as everything spirals
into the dirt

and they play as though
it's the 1950's and everything
is clear cut high and tight
horn rimmed suburban grid

while she boils alone
and the dark never lets up
and this world is fuming
fuming from within

and she only wants to scream
but her biggest fear is
what her own voice
would sound like

holding

she'd shoot herself in the foot
if it were all that easy

so she'll settle for this
counterfeit self sabotage

hoping for anything to
pull her up
or drag her down

anything but this
anything

dust

she swears she once
saw a reason in all of this

some promise of payment
some justification
for all of this

but the days
the years
grind on
each harder
often more unbearable
than the last

and she's beginning to wonder
if there really will be any
reconciliation

or is this all there is

spending a lifetime
melting into nothing

until all that's left
is a husk
that no one will miss
when the fickle wind
finally blows it away

allergen

with apologies to Les Claypool

she stares point blank
down the cavernous barrel
or tomorrow's threatening sunrise

anything but more
because it's all she can do
to suck in the next breath

the floor seems fitting
and sometimes she even
allows herself it

a concrete truth
self rectifying machine
bent on nothing but
returning everything
to its baseline zero

the dust and hair that
collects by the baseboards
sometimes finds its way
into her nostrils in the night

but that am congestion
if nothing else
is confirmation
that at least her meat
still wants to move

realization

she continues to sit alone
recycling a past that
never had to happen
in the first place

everything hurts in these days
these nights of nothing
but regret and
all the losses
so many
it seems impossible for
time to allow so much

but here she is,
alone
cold
hopeless
shivering the nights away
with the dread that
this is all there ever was

bookends

she's searching for an ending

something to bring this down
rake it into the eternal over

this but not everything

she wants what it's all become
to finally fall into the abyss
of the forever forgotten

but from that canyon
she wants a flower of what will be
to sprout heavenly

and it's okay if it's only a single stalk
in fact maybe that's preferrable
she imagines seeing the
beauty in simplicity

she wants it
needs it
and hopes for it
every night

she she's searching for an ending

but not
the end

and maybe tomorrow
she'll find it

in search of technicolor

streets are always cold

she can't rightly explain
why she does this

at least once a week
forces herself onto a world
that painfully obviously
is oblivious if not
outright hostile
to her existence

the faces blank her
or at best look away
in a misplaced courteousness
trying their hardest
to mask their contempt

she feels slow in these moments
and it's not like the
downtown moonlight reflecting off
the glistening sidewalk puddles
kind of slow motion

not anything like
childhood movies promised

but still she does this
because despite everything she knows
everything life has taught her to be true
she wants to believe
the there is life
in the midnight atmosphere

the coin

so many decisions
she faulters and flaws
trying her hardest to
recognize the real from the
totally inconsequential

a world of burning uncertainty
clasped ever tighter
in the vise of her own
best intentions

if stress headaches were the worst
this world would be
something else

papers flutter across her desk
as nameless existences
flounder this way and that
unbeknownst to an
indifferent galaxy
that will go on existing
without the divine interference
of the human hand

apart

she's trying to keep it together
doesn't know what she needs
but she knows this isn't it
this fledgling repetition
this painful banality

she's trying to keep it together
but most days if feels like
there's no choice
but to fall apart

more dust

she pretends to remember a time
when all of this monotony
didn't seem so preordained
tries to fool herself into believing
that there was once a moment
when although nothing was right
there was a wistful hope of
regaining her perpetually shaky equilibrium

there is a thick layer of dust
on top of the tv
and exponentially more
on the windowsill
nothing is clean anymore
everything so far gone
any kind of restoration
feels like a the sickest of jokes

hope feels a like a cruel barb
something to bleed her out
as the entire world
rolls their eyes and laughs
because to them, she's not real

to herself
she wonders if she ever was

simmering

she feels the hatred
boil and bleed
bubbling up within her
a poison acid
laying claim to
what's left of her humanity

she swears to herself
tonight will be the last
tonight it will burn
so hot
radiating such evil
in the morning
nothing will be left

but the hopeful her
she thinks might've once existed
though she's not entirely sure
that's strictly true

she can't remember a time
when this bloody rage
didn't shoot her eyes red
and knot her guts
with the terror
that it may never end

exist

today she did it
because nothing ever happens

it's the same life
if that's the word
no one notices
no one cares
nothing ever changes
it's the same
blank
lonely
emptiness
absolute nothingness
in an ocean
supposedly packed to explosion
with everything

the red numbers
on the crosswalk sign
hit zero long ago
but those horns were
an acknowledgement
a validation
and as she sat
in the middle of the intersection
she almost felt something

cave

she's been living here so long
it's hard to remember a time
where sunlight was if not the rule
at least a suggestion at the ready
she likes to think herself
a bear deep in her cave
hibernating

problem is
she's got no cub, save perhaps her things
and though she's never
been on a nature hike
she doubts the average cave
reeks of mold, stale corn chips
and all the lost hope
this isolation brings

they say she's on the dole
or that's what she imagines they'd say
if they said anything about her
and that's alright
she's got herself
and she'll continue to breathe
until she doesn't
and what else could a body want

still she almost remembers a time
when it wasn't this
when there was sky
when things weren't grey and faded
when life wasn't a perpetually wet shoe

sometimes she wakes at two or four
when no one's out
unless they're up to no good
she pops open with this
niggling rat at the back of her brain
gnawing a story of color and hope
those times she almost believes
but she's seen the forecast
the clouds are here for good

options

there are mornings
nights
impenetrable seconds
when she finds breathing
all but
suffocatingly impossible

the idea of life
becomes stagnant with
any perceived past slight
a constant promise of
a falling humanity
a flailing will to be human

she sees the
bodies on the street below
thrumming with something
anything
a thing she can't fathom
this drive this patience
this perseverance

pulling the blinds
she sees those below as
kitchen appliances
mechanical pencils
sanitary napkins

inanimate and to be used
and to be eliminated
the second they've
become obsolete

she returns to her black room
tells herself
this emptiness is better

closed

she's heard tell of those
who greet a day
as an unblemished opportunity
a new way to mold
the world
and more importantly
the self
into the new

even on the most base
most intellectual
most instinctual level
she finds this viewpoint lacking

while sunlight creates a façade
a veneer of promise
she knows the truth of the atmosphere
the thickness of the air
is as oppressive as
all those faces

the heat under the blankets
is its own brand of stifling
but the solitary brings a comfort
she holds on tighter

beginner

she read somewhere
about eyes scanning the horizon

and she thinks of how
this seems like a
worthy pastime

one in which she'll never participate
because it's hard to
scan any horizon
when one is stuck behind the
drawn blinds of their
bargain bin apartment

all lights always off,
nothing to show for a
maddeningly continuing life
except dying consol television
and a broken bare mattress
flopped in the corner of a room
that is somehow the
absolute visual representation of
depression

she slides a finger between the slats
of the never dusted blinds
pulls two slightly apart

she can't see a horizon
but she supposes the spot where
the gray sky meets the
crumbling brick facade of the
building across the street
is good enough for a beginner

happy meal

she cried in the
mcdonald's drive thru today

it came out of nowhere
right in between the
chicken nugget happy meal
and the diet cola

it all came boiling over
and she sat sobbing
out the window
cars honking behind
befuddled minimum wage kid
on the other side of the speaker

a solid forty five seconds of wails
that seemed like all afternoon

then she wiped snot
on the back of her hand
did her best to pretend
nothing had happened
pulled forward
paid the kid

collecting her greasy paper bag
at the second window

she asked the teenager
on the other side
if maybe she could get
some extra napkins

cut

if only there were some way
to give up this
overwhelming hatred
of herself

she boils and stews
alone all nights
feeling the poison acid
eating and destroying
building nothing from something

and it's been going on so long
she has trouble remembering
what it was like before
if there ever really was before

alone and dark
she feels it
burrowing in
constantly making her
less than she ever imagined

there was a moment
brief as it was
hazy and bordering on gone
as it was
when she was free of all this

more than that
this never existed
so
there was nothing from which
to be freed

she thinks on this time
with fond reverence
and disdain
and everything else
because definitions have become
fuzzy at best
and then a memory of some slight
imagined or not
returns
and she's back to the races

she knows no end to this circle
without severing the snake's head

mute wheel

she sees everything
beyond the edge
of a shattered day

lost moments of
missing thoughts
almost felt
but then gone
drifting past her nose
reminding her of
what could have been
what should have been

everything is cold
and unforgiving
and if nothing else
she feels a strange oneness
with all of this unsettling wrong

discomfort has become
familiar to the point of
being almost comfortable

so she moves on
plowing through yesterdays
that looks suspiciously
like tomorrow

and last year
shouts into the future

a scream comes from somewhere
and she praises to the point of cursing
her traitor mouth

accumulation

searching for the
beautiful silence
in the chaos of this
perpetually blemished world
she finds the dust
collecting in the cracks
of the worn floorboards
to be something of a comfort

in the way some may
wake to find a blanket
of new fallen snow on a day
with no travel plans
to be a promise of cozy bliss

not all of that dust
was there yesterday
and unless she intervenes
more will be there tomorrow

it's proof of the potential of growth
how something can become more
given time
and momentum

she goes to the greying sheet
that serves as a curtain

looks to the street
and for a moment
she can see herself out there
swaying with the other bodies
in the civilized dance of society

worth it

another fall south
she finds grease
on the floor

the collective dander of life
fuzz everything contaminated

she thinks of the
world above the floor

it doesn't seem worth it

stasis

she feels herself
frozen to the floor
where she woke up again
for no reason other than
she simply didn't
have it in her to
make it to the bed
again

anything feels like
more effort than this life
could ever warrant
and there's always the
faint unspoken hope
that she won't wake up

early hours
as sunlight tiptoes
into the day
she wonders what it
would be like to
stumble upon herself
sprawled and gone
then she gets up
goes to the day
and gets on with
killing time

because none it matters
especially not
her fantasies

accelerate cycle

she finds ways
too keep it moving

functioning on squeaking wheels
and grinding gears

she knows one day
the works will explode
and on that day
what's left of her
will go with it

she's felt the tremble
of faltering machinery
knows the smell
of a dying engine

but all the existential
blue smoke in creation
won't keep her from
pushing on

until oblivion
reclaims her

part

she finds herself
wishing she could admit
and accept that
everything is going to fall
and there's nothing
she or anyone else
can do about it

but the pointlessness of everyday
grinds and grates in a way
that assures her
the scars have purpose

she blows out the last candle
thinking tomorrow
maybe the clouds will part

wandering wondering

some nights she
works her feet to uselessness
walking the endless
pointless streets
wandering
searching for anything
that will bring something
of a purpose

cold drizzle under heels
her mind races at speeds
her legs could never match

some nights she walks
until the sun becomes visible
on the tree line
just outside of town
and she wonders if
that answer is in the orange
light that's always
just out of reach

she dreams of rattlesnakes

she dreams of rattlesnakes
they slide their way in
darkness
silence
except when she needs a little percussion

she dreams of rattlesnakes
they wrap around her at night
a cool dry reminder
of what it's like to breathe

she dreams of rattlesnakes
they come when the moon is high
when the sky is clear
when her mind needs them the most

she dreams of rattlesnakes
they've got teeth
but the poison only comes
when she wants it
or needs it
or only wants to taste a little death again
just to make sure she's still breathing

she dreams of rattlesnakes
their scales against her skin
their breath

their tongues
hotter than anything the sun could show

she dreams of rattlesnakes
and they will come
they always do
but morning always comes too
and it's always
so painfully mammalian

char

she's staring out the window again
watching a world that
categorically
definitively
doesn't belong to her

seeing the effortless
waterlike
airlike flow

but the shimmer of that simple ease
has spent decades dulling in her eyes
and she no longer yearns
to feel what she imagines they must

they've transferred from a goal
a heaven
to some obtuse experiment
cells under a microscope
or ants beneath a magnifying glass

and she can no longer lie to herself
and pretend she wouldn't enjoy
watching them all cook

the path

remembering all those
noxious yesterdays
burning holes
in all that's left
she wonders how
she was able to get
even this far
short trek that it is

she'd like to
thank a god
or pure grit
or anything other than
dumb luck
but all signs
point to chance
all fingers
lead to a lack of substance

she chews her life
with the same vigor
she reserves for
reheated ramen

she knows there's
something more
but she's becoming

increasingly terrified that
her chance has been
dead and rotting
since when she was
obliviously sleepwalking
through her final shot

every day's a new mystery

there's blood under her fingernails
and she's not sure how it got there

not like it's something she forgot
a detailed few seconds
in a scrap of a night that was
blown away in fists

there is no discernible cause
no precipitation for the maroon crust
drying and flaking under her
ragged and chipped nails

she strains her mind for
something resembling a reason
some kind of narrative that will
bring her to the satisfying conclusion
of why

but all she can think of is how
this is not right

she pulls the blanket over her head
tomorrow she'll deal with this

as the midnight begins to claim her
she wonders if there's an
extra toothbrush in the bathroom

she waits at the window

she waits at the window
time passes
passes
passes
she doesn't notice

she waits at the window
days are days
but this is life
this is real
this is all

she waits at the window
it will all make sense
it will
all things will eventually
add up

she waits at the window
and life keeps extrapolating
for everyone
but her

translucent

you're not invisible
she tells herself
from the safety of the
inside of her lone window

once the thought
would have terrified her
knowing that people can see
should they choose

but now the knowing
that if she were to
open the blinds
if she were to
walk down to the streetcorner
eyes would meet hers

there would be recognition
if not proving
then at least suggesting
that she in fact is human

and not this scarred
scared thing she sees
in the rare events when she
eschews all judgment
and looks in the bathroom mirror

you're not invisible
she tells herself

someone down on the sidewalk
waves toward her building

from her darkened apartment
high above street level
she waves back

some tomorrow

she thinks on
giving it a name
if for no other reason
than to put a word to this
unrelenting, nauseous churning
that continues to burn
no matter how long
no matter how many ways
she tries to shove it down

there was a lone dove
though in hindsight it was
probably only a pigeon
outside her bedroom window yesterday

there was something about that
gentle unsuspecting cooing
that seemed to momentarily
bring her world back into
some semblance of perspective
and sinc, she hasn't relented
in seeking signs in the sky
that maybe there is something after
something beyond all this
unnamable pain

she thinks on
giving it a name
but on second thought
she decides it doesn't deserve
such niceties
not when some living thing
on the other side of the blinds and glass
could be promising her
healing is wrapped in
some tomorrow

digging

she does her best
to remember times
when it wasn't this

and she knows
it did happen
not some recurring dream
drilled into her subconscious
until it might as well
have happened

she knows there was a time
when this darkness
didn't fold itself around her
when the cloudless sky
offered everything
when the gift of breath
was one to savor

she does her best
to remember those times
but they happened so long ago
they might as well
have happened to someone else
or never at all

motion

she found ways reasons
to keep moving
though at the bottom
they always rung hollow

she kept moving
swearing that as long as
she stayed in motion
the world could not pass
without her passing
right along with it

she kept moving
and all the internal conflict
boiled molten holes in her
while everything external
crumbled and rebuilt
crumbled and rebuilt

she kept moving
until the day she didn't
and when she finally stopped
the world did not take notice

zen

she's trying her hardest
to find the zen in things
to make even the most mundane
magical in its celebration of the moment

she's trying so hard to
appreciate the way the water
flows so forcefully delicate
as she scrubs the crusted remnants
of a gas station burrito
from a plastic plate

she does her best to savor
the way the glass of water
condensates in the sweltering heat
doing her damnedest to
not wish it were beer

she's so sure there's a way
to see the beauty in how
the blue smoke from the
tailpipe of a rusted el camino
goes all centrifugal to the sky

she does her best to
ignore how that sky doesn't care
she knows this indifference in the world
and she's trying to turn a blind eye to it

but when her thumb gets caught
between hammer and nail
on what should be the most
basic of repairs
and the blood flows
and the skin goes purple
she wanders if all this oneness
is just a crock of shit

running her leaking hand
under the sputtering faucet
she knows the world outside
doesn't care

she holds her breath
and searches for the moment

current

she does her best
to let everything flow over
she is the stone
on the riverbed
or that's how she envisions it

most days though
she is the bug
sometimes floating
but usually struggling
flailing
and ultimately failing
at staying above the surface

just enough for
one
more
breath

free air should never be
so suffocating
but maybe that's how everyone feels
when the lights dim
or are just too damn bright
too much in any direction
to form a coherent thought

the daily pressure is often enough
to cause her eyes to water
and her nose to leak
and she lies awake wondering
if all this physically manifested agony
is not somehow deserved

she remembers when
a cup of tea
in a chipped ceramic mug
and an early night with the mattress
were enough to set things at rights
at least for a while

now the specter of existence
has gained such momentum
she can't imagine
anything so weak and ordinary
being able to drown it all

evening grass whispers yesterdays

she's got this locket
and she's sure it
meant something
to someone once
but that meaning
has gotten lost
in the mud and the years
and no small amount of
sweetly mown grass

pictures faded to
little more than pulp
brass tarnished to
scrapyard metal
she stands in the field,
thinks of all that locket
once contained
the hopes and fears
loves and disappointments
triumphs and ultimate
final failures

dime store trumpery
or treasured heirloom
in the end it doesn't matter
because the sun is going red
and the grass is going to seed
and the significance
is all hers

unmovable

she's been trying her damndest to come at each day
with something approaching renewed purpose
most days if not all she's sickeningly aware
that it's little more than self deception

but in her book this new book
all those little lies are okay if they get her through
another always just one more
and then another, and another

she's been stacking up days
like the woodpile she vaguely remembers
from some childhood camping trip
and just like that seemingly endless wall of logs

these days are beginning to seem
potentially endless in their promise
this newfound cautious optimism
often feels odd on her;

hanging off her bones
like the ill fitted suit of forced cheeriness that it is
but she tells herself to
fake it until she makes it

and each morning she forces herself
from the bare mattress on the bare floor
that first log of the day is laid
square and true and soon to be unmovable

James Benger is the author of several books of poetry and prose. He serves on the Board of Directors of the Writers Place and the Riverfront Readings Committee, and is the founder of the 365 Poems in 365 Days online workshop. He lives in Kansas City with his wife and children.

This project was made possible, in part, by generous support from the Osage Arts Community.

Osage Arts Community provides temporary time, space and support for the creation of new artistic works in a retreat format, serving creative people of all kinds — visual artists, composers, poets, fiction and nonfiction writers. Located on a 152-acre farm in an isolated rural mountainside setting in Central Missouri and bordered by ¾ of a mile of the Gasconade River, OAC provides residencies to those working alone, as well as welcoming collaborative teams, offering living space and workspace in a country environment to emerging and mid-career artists. For more information, visit us at www.osageac.org